EDMUND+OCTAVIA

A Better Lie

18 Life Lessons from the Game of Golf

Kerry J Charles

EDMUND+OCTAVIA

A BETTER LIE Copyright © 2016 Kerry J Charles. All rights reserved, including the right to reproduce this book or portions thereof in any form whatsoever. In accordance with the U.S. Copyright Act of 1976, the scanning, uploading, and electronic sharing of any part of this book without the permission of the publisher is unlawful piracy and theft of the author's intellectual property. If you would like to use material from the book (other than for review purposes), prior written permission must be obtained by contacting the author at Edmund+Octavia Publishing at EdmundOctavia.com.

Illustrations from *Pictorial Golf* by H.B. Martin, available from Edmund+Octavia publishing.

ISBN-10: 0-9963393-4-5
ISBN-13: 978-0-9963393-4-6

Edmund+Octavia Publishing, Falmouth, ME

CONTENTS

1	**A Better Lie** *Know when you just need to do the right thing.*	1
2	**Club Selection** *Analyze your options, then go with your gut.*	5
3	**Laying Up** *Know your limits and have the courage* *to acknowledge them.*	9
4	**Aim Beyond the Hole** *Dream bigger.*	13
5	**The Bump and Run** *Pretty doesn't matter if it gets the job done.*	17
6	**Hit the Sand, Not the Ball** *The direct approach isn't always the best idea.*	21
7	**In the Rough** *Face your demons.*	25
8	**The Drop Zone** *You don't always need to push yourself.* *It's okay to work from your comfort zone.*	29
9	**Playing Off the Mat** *Learn how to temper yourself when required.*	33
10	**The Long Drive** *Be comfortable with the outcome of a calculated risk.*	37
11	**Putting Uphill is Easier** *Quick doesn't necessarily mean better.*	41
12	**Care Less. Focus More.** *Stop worrying about the outcome.* *Pay attention to what you're doing now.*	45
13	**Swing Your Own Swing** *Do what you do best and have faith that it will work.*	49
14	**Loosen the Grip** *Lighten up and stop trying to control everything.*	53
15	**Penalty Strokes** *Acknowledge your mistake and* *take your punishment gracefully.*	57
16	**Hiring a Caddie** *There are times when you can't go it alone.*	61
17	**Scrambling** *Accept adversity and carry on.*	65
18	**The Ace** *Make your own luck.*	69

Preface

I took up golf at the tender age of 47, decades after most players have lifted a club for the first time. Prior to that I'd thought it was a silly game. Hit a ball with a stick and chase it around until it gets into the hole. That's how most non-players see the game.

Once I started, I learned how addictive golf can be, and it's all because of those elusive fantastic hits. Strike the ball well just once and you know, deep in your heart, that you can certainly do it again. That's what keeps golfers going.

Golf is an inherently contemplative game. It can't be hurried. It's quiet. It promotes a great deal of thought. That's where this book came from. The more I learned about playing golf, the more I realized how it paralleled life. I doubt I would have recognized this if I hadn't lived half a lifetime already before starting the game.

I've enjoyed writing this book and sharing my thoughts with other golfers. I hope you enjoy reading it.

~ Kerry J Charles

A Better Lie

Know when you just need to do the right thing.

Imagine hitting a nearly perfect drive. You walk along happily, spotting your ball ahead only slightly in the rough. As you come closer, you see that it's landed a mere two inches from a small tuft of grass. An inviting small tuft of grass. You eye it, picturing your ball sitting gently on top. It would be just high enough for the sweet spot of your three wood to nuzzle up perfectly beside it, waiting for you to swing effortlessly, making contact with that delightful sound, half way between a click and a clink. You would easily be on the green.

It's a dilemma that has faced many a golfer the world over. A better lie.

A BETTER LIE

It's a simple question: do you pick up the ball and place it where you can hit it more easily, or do you try to hit it as it lies? Deep in their hearts, every golfer knows the true answer to this question: moving the ball is cheating.

But let's face it. We're not all professional golfers. We just want to play a good round. And isn't it in the interest of everyone to maintain a steady pace of play and not stand there hacking at a ball that's stuck in a divot or buried in the rough? So we pick up the ball and place it where we can hit it more easily. A better lie.

The better lie is simply about you and your conscience. If you're playing a round just for fun, then it's easy. Pick up the ball and place it where you're more apt to strike it well. If you're playing a practice round, then it's up to you whether you want to practice a good lie or a bad one. But if you're playing with others for a score, for money, for tournament glory, then picking up the ball and placing it for a better lie is unacceptable. Even if no one sees you do it.

We've all cut corners in our lives. We've all told little fibs or done the wrong thing just to make the game of life easier. We hit the accelerator when the light turns yellow. We sneak an extra cookie. We pretend that we've spent the afternoon mowing the lawn when in fact we hired the kid next door to do it while we sit on the couch watching the golf channel. We've all placed that proverbial ball in a better spot.

The question to ask yourself is: does this subtle bit of cheating negatively affect anyone else, or is it just making things better for you? If it only affects you and you can sleep at night having made the choice, go for it. No harm done.

But if that nagging little voice at the back of your mind tells you that your words or actions might not be quite the right thing, well then, you know what you should do. Play the ball as it lies.

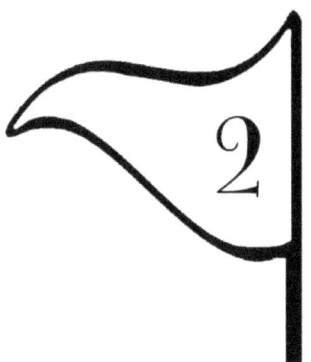

Club Selection

Analyze your options, then go with your gut.

Every golfer knows that one of the key reasons to spend time at the driving range is to learn, with as much precision as possible, how far each club will send the ball sailing out over the fairway. To make matters more complicated, any given club is different in the hands of any given golfer. The ball may reach 150 yards with a 7 iron for you, but put that same club in the hands of someone else and it may only take the ball 120 yards.

Of course we also need to factor in many other influences such as the weather, the ball's lie, and the golfer's general level of fitness for any particular day (that right elbow has just been stiff lately). Now the 7 iron might only take the ball 135 yards. Which leaves us with a choice. Do we reach for the 6 iron instead?

Many golfers have tried to make club selection into a science. Certainly science is involved. The speed that the club moves, the angle that it strikes the ball, the wind, the humidity – all of these factors can be accounted for. Club selection should be easy. We see the pros analyzing shots with their caddies, consulting their notes and poring over yardage books. They make it look like a science.

Yet the pros that make it look easy have one thing in common. They all seem to have a mystical sixth sense for what will work. Sure they get it wrong sometimes, but ask any of them why they used a particular club on a particular shot and, after giving you the analysis, they'll add, "… plus, it just felt right."

If you've played (and practiced) golf for long enough, you'll know that you just get a sense for what will work. You might be wrong. (Okay, you'll be wrong fairly often.) But usually you'll have a gut feeling for the right club at the right time. Analysis helps to narrow our choices. It brings is to a decision between a 7 iron and a 6 iron. But that final choice doesn't come from our brain. It comes from a gut feeling of what will work.

Everyone who golfs has uttered the words, "I knew I should have used the other club!" That phrase, *I knew I should have…*, sums up more regret in people's lives than perhaps any other. There are numerous options for finishing that sentence: *…brought an umbrella, …ordered the steak, …taken the other road.* We second-guess ourselves far too often.

Put all the careful thought into a decision that you want. Consider every possible angle and variable if that makes you more comfortable. Factor in all of the possibilities. When you're done, file it all away in your brain and then just go with your gut.

Laying Up

Know your limits and have the courage to acknowledge them.

Angel Cabrera famously said, "I didn't lay up when I was poor. Why would I start now?" Time and time again we see the pros pull out the driver and go for the green. They'll reach for the three wood to rip it over the water hazard rather than choosing the iron that would safely place the ball in that very large space of short grass over on the side. We all cheer when they achieve glory with the big club.

But what about when they miss? No one wants to think about that. Why would you? You've decided to go for it, eschewing those wimpy little irons, carefully lining up your shot. In your mind you can see it, soaring like a condor over the water hazard below, then landing with a resounding plunk on the green exactly pin-high. Of course you'll make it. Sure.

So you do it. Throw caution to the wind. And then you watch in horror as your ball falls short and makes that spectacular splash, never to be seen again (by you, anyway).

Laying up has become the equivalent of wimping out. Real men and women don't lay up. Golf isn't just about scoring low, it's about showing off with the glory shot, right? Ask the pros, however (with the possible exception of Mr. Cabrera although he would probably concur in the end) and they'll tell you: the only thing that matters is the final score. It's all fun and games for the rest of us but for the pros, that's their paycheck.

They know when to lay up. They have the courage to acknowledge their own limits, to know their own game. That kind of self-knowledge can apply to just about anything. Maybe it isn't quite the time yet to get that Porsche while you're still paying off the college loans. The law degree might be fine for your sister, but maybe you'll be lots happier (and possibly more successful in the long run) by sticking with graphic design.

Knowing your limitations doesn't mean that they're limiting. On the contrary, by knowing and accepting them, we can work with and around them to achieve our goals.

You carry a lot of different clubs in your bag for a reason: each and every one is useful at a different time. Don't be afraid to pull out an iron. You might not hear the roaring crowd just then, but when you reach the end with a score that's better than everyone else's, finding success on your terms, you'll be the hero at the 18th green.

Aim Beyond the Hole
Dream Bigger.

One-hundred percent of all putts that fall short of the hole will not go in. Everyone knows that. Yet how many times have you failed to hit the ball hard enough to reach the cup?

Golfers vary on how much farther they aim beyond the hole. Some follow a slower path that works with any potential break but will still put them slightly beyond the hole if they miss. Others take the firm approach with harder contact, leaving little doubt that they'll get to the hole and beyond. When they miss, they may have a longer putt back, but they're confident in making it since they've just seen the break as the ball made its way past the cup.

The whole point of aiming beyond the hole, however, is to make sure that you've given yourself at least a chance of sinking the ball. If you don't even reach the cup, you'll never have that chance.

Coming up short is something that we all do in life. We watch wistfully as others achieve their dreams, reach their goals, as they score big. We wonder why we can't do the same.

If we don't set our goals high enough, we may not be giving ourselves the opportunity to meet them. What if your goal is to write a book? That's great, but maybe you should adjust that goal to writing not just a book, but a best-seller. Not only will you be focused on writing the book, but you'll be pushing yourself to make it that much better – more thorough, more accurate, more thrilling, as the case may be. Now you have something bigger to work toward, something perhaps more inspiring and exciting. You may not achieve the bestseller list, but you'll almost certainly have met your first goal: to write a book.

It's human nature to stop when we think the job is done. Those extra credit questions on a test often go unanswered. But what if they were actually part of the test and you didn't know it? You'd then have the chance to get an A+ without getting everything right.

Whatever it is that you want to achieve, dream bigger. Aim for the next higher goal. You may not reach it, but by setting your sights beyond, you're giving yourself a much better chance of fulfilling the original dream.

The Bump and Run
Pretty doesn't matter if it gets the job done.

You've hit your third shot on a par five just short of the green. You're in the fairway, but a gentle upward slope separates you from the fringe. You pull out your wedge thinking you'll chip it up near the hole, then putt in for par. Easy.

Any number of disasters could strike at this point, though. You might land the ball on the downslope behind the pin, at which point it rolls off the green. Or you put a bit of backspin on it that you didn't intend, it falls short of the cup, then maddeningly returns toward you. In your mind, however, this never happens. The ball arcs gracefully into the air, lands near the cup and perhaps rolls right in.

Chipping can get you where you need to be with precision. Plus, when it's done well, it's pretty darned impressive. It can also get you into loads of trouble very quickly. Chipping requires control over the ball not only while it's in the air, but also after it lands on the ground.

The bump and run may be a better option. The advantage of this shot is that, like a putt, you can see where the ball will be travelling. You can carefully look at the grass, the slope leading up to the fringe, and see the undulations of the green. You can imagine how the ball will move from your club to the hole.

For most golfers, the chip shot is more daunting. More can go wrong, and if that happens, the recovery is usually more difficult. The bump and run may not be as exciting (let's face it – it's usually just downright ugly), but the chances are greater that you'll get the ball at least close to the hole.

Golf is a game of numbers, and you want as few as possible. If that means using a club in an unorthodox way or opting for a shot that isn't quite the norm, it doesn't matter. Your scorecard won't care.

Most people don't want to look silly. You'll be laughed at. It's important to fit in, to look and act like those around you. To keep up with the proverbial Jonses.

What we might not realize, however, is that in trying to look the part, we're risking shooting above par. How many people have bought the Lexus when they couldn't really afford it because everyone else had one. Or taken the vacation that wasn't first on their list because that's what their brother-in-law was doing.

The point is to know what works for you, go with it, and not worry about how it might appear. Know when life's little 'bump-and-runs" will make things easier for you and get the job done, regardless of how they might look to everyone else.

Hit the Sand, Not the Ball
The direct approach isn't always the best idea.

The dreaded bunker. Not the fairway bunker, but the bunker right next to the green. The bunker next to the green that has a three-foot wall separating you from the green itself. You can spot the top of the flagstick, but actually seeing the hole is out of the question.

With more than a little trepidation you step down in with your trusty sand wedge. You frantically try to remember what you're supposed to do. Club face open. Turn your body. Follow through. And the number-one key to the elusive bunker shot: don't hit the ball, hit the sand.

You've spent the vast majority of your round attempting to hit the ball in as many ways possible to get just the right angle, speed, trajectory, spin... now you're not supposed to hit it at all. It seems crazy.

Crazy, but it works. That amazing sand wedge is designed so that the bottom of it can bounce right into the sand, shoving it against your ball, and rocketing it out of that dastardly bunker. Your club hits the sand and the sand shoves the ball.

It's an indirect approach that works, and that's the whole point. A regular club would most likely dig into the sand and cause no end of trouble immediately. The sand wedge happily thumps along the top of the sand, pushing the surface up and your ball along with it.

The indirect approach. It can be more powerful, yet paradoxically easier, than the direct approach. Perhaps your spouse is wearing a shirt that looks like a throwback from the seventies. You could say, "That's the ugliest shirt I've ever seen," and risk his annoyance along with that endearing trait of digging in his heels, in which case you're stuck seeing the shirt for the rest of the evening. Or you could say, "I love that blue shirt you have. You really look great in it – I was hoping you'd wear it," at which point there's a high degree of probability that he'll go change.

The direct approach can often sound like criticism. No one really enjoys that. It can be a verbal tidal wave of negativity washing over you. The indirect approach, however, is often couched in a suggestion. The focus is the end game rather than the current conflict.

The indirect approach works well when delivering bad news. Bad news such as, "Looks like you're in the bunker again!" The next time your golf buddy hits one in the sand, just say, "Hey, now's your chance to show us all up with that new sand wedge!" They'll thank you for it.

In the Rough
Face your demons.

Everyone who has played golf at least once has probably hit the ball in the rough. Of course, this means that you have to hit the ball out of the rough. You might have to search for it first, scuffling through the taller grass, secretly hoping you don't find it. But there it is. Nestled down in, mocking you.

It's annoying, and your first instinct is to take the same club that you would use for that distance on the fairway and just whack the hell out of it. The goal is the same after all, right?

Not necessarily. Think about the design of your clubs. They're made to hit the ball on short grass, to create spin, to maximize trajectory and distance. They are not designed to wade into a thicket of weeds. Even if you manage to strike the ball cleanly, you'll most likely get the club head caught immediately after, inhibiting your follow-through.

Once you're in the rough, your goal has temporarily changed. It is not to get the ball in the hole. The goal now to get the ball out of the rough. Sure, you can still move in the general direction of the hole – that's encouraged. But your primary focus is to get out of the rough as quickly as possible.

How do we accomplish this? It's pretty straightforward: analyze the rough. Determine exactly how your ball is positioned (high or plugged?), the kind of vegetation that is surrounding it (thick and tough or easily broken?), and the direction that the grass is growing (against your swing or toward it?). By looking carefully at the ball's situation you greatly improve your chances of getting it out of that situation, then you can return to your original goal of moving the ball forward, toward the cup.

Goals are fantastic. The help us move our lives forward. They give us a sense of accomplishment. They're the yummy carrot hanging on the stick that keeps us going.

Life can get in the way, however. Setbacks abound. That broken arm is not going to help you break eighty this year, or probably even next.

Major goals don't have to change, but there are times when we do need to adjust them and focus on something different temporarily. Your goal with your broken arm is to get out of the cast as quickly as possible, then to build up strength. At that point you can start thinking about breaking eighty again.

Goals are beset by the demons of life. They make us want to give up. Yet, by facing those demons head on, by analyzing them and determining how to cut them loose and get out of the rough, they're overcome more efficiently. Once that happens, we're back on the short grass making our way forward to the hole.

The Drop Zone

You don't always need to push yourself. It's okay to work from your comfort zone.

You've just hit a spectacularly terrible shot, straight into the water hazard. The splash was photo-worthy. You now have a choice: try again and risk the same frustrating result, or hit from the drop zone.

The dreaded drop zone. Just standing in that circle seems to suck the confidence out of you. It's the golf equivalent of wearing a dunce cap. In many ways, hitting from the drop zone induces more nerves than teeing off – once you're in that circle, missing the shot is inexcusable, beyond embarrassing.

Still, you choose to hit from the zone. You walk around it from the outside, considering the shot. There's something about stepping inside that circle that feels like a commitment, even before you've actually dropped ball. You select your club, and taking a deep breath, in you go.

The rest is automatic. Hold your arm out shoulder high, drop the ball. Line up your shot, go through your normal routine and breathe a sigh of relief when your ball hits the green.

Although it may feel a little like cheating (except that you've already been penalized), the drop zone is there for a reason. You can make it from there. It's a comfort zone. It allows you to regroup and get back in the game.

We all have a comfort zone but many of us feel as though working from there is cheating. In today's culture, we're supposed to push ourselves, right? We're told to step "outside of the box" and force ourselves to try new things. While that's a great way to promote personal growth, remember to use it wisely because it will, by definition, make you uncomfortable.

Your comfort zone is comfortable for a reason: you're good at working within it. You've had a lot of practice inside that zone. You are the expert of whatever is in your own comfort zone.

Everyone undervalues their own expertise, their own talents. If it comes easily to you, you assume it's easy for everyone else too. Not so. You've worked very, very hard to be good at something. While stepping outside of it and pushing ourselves gives us new directions and challenges, it's the comfort zone that allows us to work toward them.

Whether you realize it or not, your comfort zone allows you to excel and accelerate. It gives you back your confidence. It's your own personal drop zone where you even get to place the ball exactly where you want it with the perfect lie and the perfect angle so that you can hit the perfect shot. With that, and a little bit of luck, you'll hole it with ease.

Playing Off the Mat
Learn how to temper yourself when required.

It's easier to get a tee time for the Old Course at St. Andrews in the winter because, let's face it, we're in Scotland in the winter. The days are short. The weather can be brutal. But still, it's the Old Course.

There is one caveat. You must play off a mat. We've all seen it – that square of plastic, artificial turf with the overly green grassy color. Usually it's found at the driving range offering a somewhat less than inviting, but still tolerable, golf experience.

Maintaining the Old Course at St. Andrews is a daunting prospect and kudos to those who make it so wonderful. That hideous mat helps keep it that way, sparing it from divots that could take weeks to heal made by winter golfers. Everyone playing the course must carry the mat with them. Following each shot a player must remove the ball, position the mat as closely as possible to where the ball was, place the ball on top of the mat, then hit. The mat must be used for each and every fairway stroke.

Why would anyone find this system acceptable for five months out of every year? Because we all know that the Old Course is important. The Old Course is fragile. Especially so during the winter months.

Many situations in life are fragile. A good friend is fighting a difficult illness. A colleague is going through a bitter divorce. Your spouse is trying to lose twenty pounds. An unmindful comment or action that normally might be forgotten by the next conversation could instead gouge a divot in their psyche.

Learn how to recognize when those around you might be more sensitive, might take longer than usual to heal, and adjust accordingly. Put down that proverbial mat before you say or do anything around them. Chances are good that by springtime when the grass can grow again and the fairway has healed, all will be well.

The Long Drive
Be comfortable with the outcome of a calculated risk.

A very long par five. With a dogleg. You can't see the pin and it probably wouldn't matter if you could. You need to shorten this hole so that you even have a chance of hitting the green in three. There's only one thing to do: take out the driver, grip it and rip it.

The average drive accuracy for the top 200 players on the PGA tour is somewhere around 60%. A very few players have flirted with a 75% average. Most fall within the 50-60% range.

Think about that. These are the best players in the game, and they only drive the ball in the fairway on nine to eleven holes during the average round.

Why would they accept what seems like a relatively low percentage? Why not strive for a bit more accuracy? Why flirt with disaster by hitting the ball so hard that they lose some control over the outcome? Because they're willing to deal with that outcome, even when it's bad.

It's all about calculated risk. The pros know that they'll hit the fairway at least half the time and probably more. When they don't, they're often not too far off into the rough. Only a small percentage of their drives are completely unplayable. The risk of that is worth the reward of a drive that outdistances their opponents.

Everyone has a different tolerance for risk. Some have no problem betting every last penny while others put their hard-earned dollars in a nice, safe savings account. But life doesn't always favor those who simply save, and risk doesn't always involve money.

Taking a vacation is a calculated risk. You've planned and perhaps pre-paid for much of it, but there's always that glitch that costs more, or that lucky break that doesn't (think: first-class upgrade!). Having a child is another calculated risk. You can plan, save, go through genetic testing, and be militant about proper nutrition, yet there's still a chance that your child could be different. Whether it's a debilitating birth defect or a kid so gifted that Harvard accepts them at age twelve, you're taking a calculated risk. Nothing is certain, so learn to be comfortable with metaphorically winning, losing or ending up somewhere in between.

Accept risk. Nothing is completely within your control. Take a few moments and imagine all possible outcomes for any decision, then move forward. But also remember that regardless of the level of risk, sometimes you just have to grip it and rip it, and hope for the best.

Putting Uphill is Easier
Quick doesn't necessarily mean better.

The greens are playing as fast as you've ever seen, and you've managed to land your ball uphill of the hole. There's at least one break between the ball and the cup. Aim wrong or swing too hard, and it could spell disaster. Your only real choice is to send down a depth charge, a nice lagged putt that will probably come close but almost certainly won't go in. That's okay – you'll still make par.

Your buddy, on the other hand, is the same distance away but downhill of the hole, and grinning while happily marking the ball, almost certain of a birdie. The uphill putt will be much easier to make.

Why is this? The distance is the same. The slope and potential break looks pretty much the same. Why would your putt be so much more difficult?

The answer is speed. It's a tricky thing. That little rolling ball will increase in speed as it moves downhill. Your putt is rocketing along whereas your buddy's putt is inching uphill at a comfortable pace, slowing down as it moves. It's easier to control something moving slowly than quickly.

Lewis Carroll's famous White Rabbit from *Alice in Wonderland* said, "The hurrier I go, the behinder I get." We live in a world that values speed: fast food, quick stock market trades, express checkout lanes at the grocery store. Yet in our quest to save time, what if we're actually losing some control? What if we're sending the trajectory of our lives off in a direction that will take us even more time to correct? What if we're just creating an extra putt for ourselves?

Maybe one question to ask yourself is, "If I take the quick route now, will my chances be greater of having to correct for it later?" Does getting fast food tonight mean an extra trip to the gym tomorrow? Does that well-timed quick stock trade mean that you miss a longer-term payoff? If you use the ten-or-less express aisle at the grocery store, will you just have to go back again sooner?

Sure, fast is great in many circumstances. But in the quest for speed, take just a few extra seconds to ask yourself if you'll pay the price later. If that's the case, maybe taking some time and "putting uphill" is the better option.

Care Less. Focus More.

Stop worrying about the outcome. Pay attention to what you're doing now.

When you watch the truly great pro golfers play, do they ever look worried? Have you ever seen true apprehension with that subtle hint of fear creeping onto their faces? It's rare.

What you do see is single-minded, laser-pointed focus on the task at hand. They don't waste much time contemplating how the round will end. They don't even seem very concerned with whether they'll birdie or bogey each hole until they're on the green. Instead, they stay in the moment, centered, thinking solely about their next swing.

It's the only swing that matters. Consider how you play a game of golf. You hit the ball. It lands on the ground. You locate it, figure out which club to use and how to use it, and you hit it again. Rinse and repeat. At no time does it help to focus on even two strokes ahead.

Sure, you can plan your strategy. You can aim for a particular spot and assume (or hope) that will be the outcome. But you can't plan on that outcome. The only thing that you can plan on is the shot immediately in front of you. And the only thing that you can do to make that shot happen is to focus on how you will hit the ball at that instant, not on where the ball might land. Why? Because it will land wherever it lands. And until it lands, caring and worrying simply waste time and energy.

How many times have you worried about the outcome of something to the point where you took your mind off the task at hand? You were concerned about getting that promotion and didn't notice that your boss had sent an email asking for changes in your upcoming presentation. When you finally read the email, you had to rush to get the job done and it wasn't as good as it could have been. The promotion might now be in jeopardy.

The end game is important, but the only thing that you can affect is whatever is happening around you right at this moment. Nothing more and nothing less. Focus on the task at hand and do that to the best of your ability. The ball will land where it lands.

Swing Your Own Swing
Do what you do best and have faith that it will work.

Inbee Park's average driving distance is 250 yards, yet her swing looks like it would barely move the ball fifty. Arnold Palmer's unorthodox swing is the stuff of legend. Jim Furyk's is nothing short of miraculous given how ugly it is. Does it matter? Not in the least.

There are numerous sources, too many to count, that discuss the "proper swing." Straight left arm, cock the wrist, lead with the lower body, extend and rotate…. Do a quick internet search and you'll find literally millions of instructions on the right way to swing a golf club.

There are certainly fundamentals that are worth learning. And definitely aspects to tweak in even the best golfer's swing. But the bottom line is: swing your own swing. It it works for you, it works for you. It's irrelevant whether it looks silly or strange or downright stupid. If it works, nothing else matters.

If it works, nothing else matters. That's worth repeating. So many of us have done what others have told us to do. We've lived the lives that others expected. We've been swinging someone else's swing.

Find your own. You know what you're good at, what works best for you. Maybe it's unorthodox. Maybe you want to travel the world studying the pan-flute. You could become the foremost authority on the subject. Maybe you want to build a complete, to-scale model of Augusta National with Legos in your garage. You would have golfers around the world paying homage to your genius. And probably literally paying to see it.

One secret to the success of swinging your own swing is having faith that it will work. The other secret is that you are the one who does it best. Better than anyone else. Don't change a thing.

Loosen the Grip
Lighten up and stop trying to control everything.

When people are new to the game of golf they typically make one mistake immediately: they grip the club too tightly. It's an honest mistake, certainly. After all, most of the time you're trying to move the ball ahead by distances measured in multiple yardages. Hundreds, even. You'd better hit that thing with all you've got.

What beginners don't realize is that the distance that the ball travels relies on more than just the force of impact. Brute force alone won't make the ball fly out into the fairway. What's also needed is club head speed.

A BETTER LIE

Golfers come in all shapes and sizes. A large, muscular build isn't required to play the game well. What is required is the correct body motion to produce both force and speed. The strength of your grip affects this motion.

When your grip is tight, imagine what happens to your arms. They tighten up as well. If they're tight, then your shoulders are probably tense, too. Now you've just restricted the motion of your arms, shoulders, and perhaps even your whole body with this chain reaction. Your swing no longer flows into a smooth, rhythmic motion. You might still hit the ball with great force, but club head speed has been reduced.

When you loosen your grip everything else relaxes as well. Now you can twist your body, swing your arms, and snap the club head around quickly. You can't loosen up too much, obviously. You don't want the club sailing along the fairway with the ball. Let go just enough to feel your arms, shoulders, and body move with ease.

This chain reaction works just as well in the rest of your life as it does in golf. Have you ever noticed that when you try to force through a project, it never seems to go quite right? When you try to rigidly control everything, it all seems to fall apart? The secret is to stop trying so hard.

Sir Richard Branson, founder of Virgin Group, once divulged a secret to his success. He said that he hires people smarter than him, then gets out of their way. He trusts them enough that he's willing to give up his own control. He loosens the grip on his companies, allows his employees to utilize their own strength and creativity, and ends up achieving amazing success.

You are not running the world. You are in control of very little. Stop trying to pretend otherwise and life will happen more easily. Loosen the grip and you'll gain so much.

Penalty Strokes

Acknowledge your mistake and take your punishment gracefully.

It felt like the perfect drive to cut the corner of your nemesis, that dogleg right par-5, but somehow it fell short and landed somewhere in the woods. After searching to the point where your buddies are all annoyed and the group behind you is standing at the tee box staring in your direction, you give up. It's a penalty stroke.

You're annoyed. You're embarrassed. And now you're out somewhere between 50¢ and $4 (you just had to get those top-of-the-line Titleist balls), not to mention probably losing whatever bet you made with the rest of your foursome. Trying to remember the appropriate rules for playing your next shot, you pull out a new ball, make a feeble attempt at dropping it correctly, and move on with the game.

At least it isn't quite as embarrassing as what the pros go through. They call over a rules judge, discuss the situation, ask if others saw it go into the woods, mark the quasi-location of where the ball might have been, measure club lengths, and finally drop the ball (often more than once). Then they can get around to hitting it. And marking an extra shot on their card. The entire process screams, "Look at me! I just totally screwed up!"

The very name is annoying. Penalty stroke. You've been penalized, you naughty thing. It feels like detention, or being grounded, or having mom yell at you because you broke her favorite vase throwing the football around indoors. And now it's right there, in black and white, on your scorecard.

Everyone gets it wrong sometimes. And everyone feels like they're getting it wrong more than anyone else. You're not. But there are times when you definitely are getting it wrong, and when that happens, acknowledge whatever it is that you did wrong and take your punishment gracefully.

No one likes a sore loser, in sports or in life. Even if you do have a good explanation, it will always end up sounding like an excuse. The bottom line is, you were wrong. If it's a mistake on the job, in your marriage, with your best friend, or even a total stranger, acknowledge what you did, take the penalty stroke, and move on.

Hiring a Caddie

There are times when you can't go it alone.

If you've ever golfed with a caddie, you'll know what a life-changing experience it can be. That might be overstating it a little, but the ease of walking an entire 18 holes free from your clubs, yet somehow having them magically appear whenever you need them, is hard to overestimate.

Beyond a human pack-mule, however, a good caddie is a wealth of knowledge. They know the course. They've seen it change with the weather. They've witnessed the good shots and the bad. They even know the subtle undulations of the greens that relate to all of those baffling pin placements.

The best caddies are also psychologists. They see you getting frustrated with a slice that doesn't seem to want to go away and suggest a subtle alteration to your stance or your swing. They'll talk to you about your game, help you through the course, and keep you on track.

And most importantly, they have an uncanny ability to be able to find your ball when you've just hit in the rough for the third time in a row, then, without any judgment, hand you the exact club that you need to save par.

Everyone's lives have difficulties. Sometimes we can navigate our way through them on our own. We trudge along, clubs clanking in the bag on our backs, and doggedly smack the ball in front of us until we make it to the end.

There are times, though, when we need someone to help carry the load and point us in the right direction. Someone with local knowledge. Someone who doesn't judge us as a human being. They just help us to get through.

It's important to know when you can't go it alone. Recognize when the burden is too heavy or the problem is so complicated that you have no idea where to hit the ball. Hire an expert if need be to get you through the difficult bits in life. For just a little while, put your faith in someone else who can carry the load and help.

Scrambling

Accept adversity and carry on.

Put very simply, scrambling in golf is not making a green in regulation but still saving par (or better). Some of the best players have achieved their greatness largely due to their scrambling skills.

By definition, scrambling means that you will not be able to safely two-putt a hole. You won't have that comfortable margin of putting once, getting the ball close, then tapping it in. Scrambling adds pressure, it taxes your mental energy by forcing you to make more decisions, and, lets face it, it simply makes you feel like you're just screwing up.

However, scrambling is part of the game. No one can consistently hit greens in regulation every single time. Sure you might have that magical round where everything is perfect, but the golf gods will certainly punish you by making your next round that much worse. You'll be scrambling on practically every hole the next time you play.

As with most challenges, the first key to overcoming them is to practice. Learn the different short-range shots that are required when you don't hit the green. It sounds easy. You know it isn't.

It isn't easy because the second key to scrambling is acceptance. No one wants to accept that they just missed. No one wants to accept the fact that, although they just gave it their best effort, they still fell short. And even worse, no one wants to even acknowledge, let alone accept, that they might not have actually given it their best effort. The best scramblers in golf have learned to accept that they missed, put it behind them, and work with the situation at hand. Keep calm and carry on.

Scrambling is a form of overcoming adversity and life is full of adversity. There are days, weeks, months, that will be a struggle, when you'll feel like you can't get anything right. Accept them and keep going. Put them behind you and have faith that ultimately you're making the right decisions, moving in the right direction.

You will be required to scramble. It is part of the game, of golf and of life. The sooner you accept this, the easier it will be to deal with the pressure of your next set of life decisions, to move forward, and to par the proverbial hole. And who knows? You might even birdie once in a while, too.

The Ace
Make your own luck.

The Ace. Elusive, compelling, mesmerizing. To imagine how the ball floats effortlessly through the air then glides ever so smoothly across the green before snugly dropping into the hole beside the pin. It's the dream of every golfer.

Somewhere, somehow, someone calculated that the odds of an average amateur golfer scoring a hole-in-one on a par three are about 12,500 to 1. The odds of a professional golfer are closer to 2,500 to 1. What does this tell us?

Certainly luck is involved. But as the saying goes, you make your luck. The average professional golfer spends 6-8 hours per day practicing. Even after playing a competitive round, many will go to the driving range and continue to work on their game. It's their job, but unlike most jobs, their income every week depends on how well they have played.

The pros also pay attention to other elements that can affect where the ball ultimately comes to rest. They think about the temperature and how it affects the flight of the ball. They consider the wind and adjust their aim. They examine the green in advance to determine where to land their drive so that the ball will roll straight toward the cup. They don't just simply aim for the pin and hope for the best.

Granted, some of it is just plain luck. If it wasn't, everyone would be able to do it. But practice, adjusting for outside influences, and proper placement are the key elements that affect that luck, improving your chances exponentially.

There are so many different ways to "score an ace" in life. Landing the perfect job, hitting the bestseller's list, becoming a millionaire through your investments… everyone's metaphorical ace is different. Luck is definitely involved. The perfect job has to be available in the first place. People need to notice and like that book you've just published. Your investments need to improve in value steadily.

Consider how you could improve your chances to score that ace. What if you wanted to land your dream job? First, become an expert at whatever your field is. That's practice. Attend conferences where other people who work in your field will congregate. That's placement. Learn new skills as they evolve in your chosen line of work. That's adjustment.

Practice, placement and adjustment. Hard work and determination. Is it easy? Nope. But add these to a little old-fashioned luck, and you just might be buying everyone that celebratory round at the 19th hole.

Available from Edmund+Octavia Publishing!

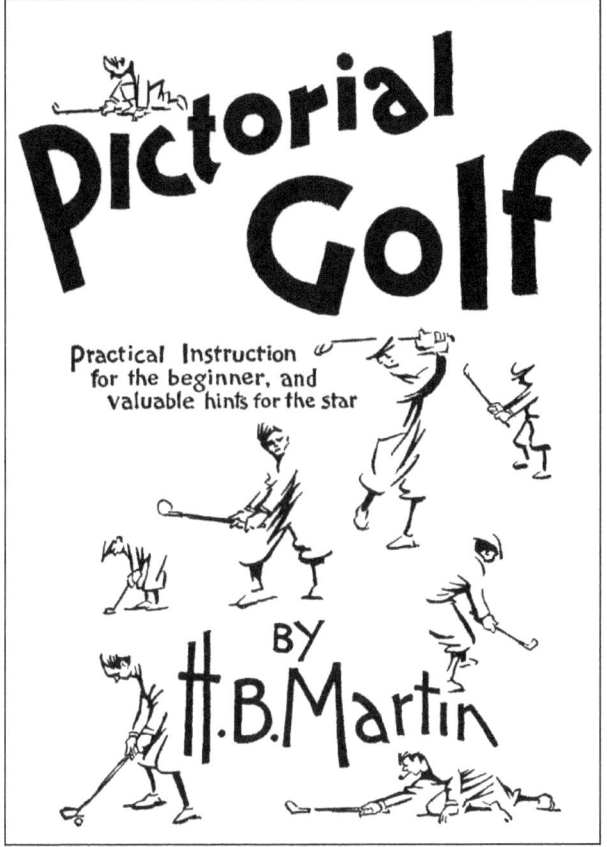

The equipment has changed thanks to technology (used your mashie niblick lately?) but physics and anatomy have not.

As relevant today as it was nearly a century ago and now digitally remastered, get the 1925 classic at booksellers online or at your local bookstore!

www.ingramcontent.com/pod-product-compliance
Lightning Source LLC
Chambersburg PA
CBHW070549300426
44113CB00011B/1840